THE
OUTER PLANETS
JUPITER, SATURN, URANUS, AND NEPTUNE

the solar system

THE
OUTER PLANETS
JUPITER, SATURN, URANUS, AND NEPTUNE

Edited by Sherman Hollar

Britannica
Educational Publishing
IN ASSOCIATION WITH
ROSEN
EDUCATIONAL SERVICES

Published in 2012 by Britannica Educational Publishing
(a trademark of Encyclopædia Britannica, Inc.)
in association with Rosen Educational Services, LLC
29 East 21st Street, New York, NY 10010.

Distributed exclusively by Rosen Educational Services.
For a listing of additional Britannica Educational Publishing titles, call toll free (800) 237-9932.

First Edition

Britannica Educational Publishing
Michael I. Levy: Executive Editor, Encyclopædia Britannica
J.E. Luebering: Director, Core Reference Group, Encyclopædia Britannica
Adam Augustyn: Assistant Manager, Encyclopædia Britannica

Anthony L. Green: Editor, Compton's by Britannica
Michael Anderson: Senior Editor, Compton's by Britannica
Sherman Hollar: Associate Editor, Compton's by Britannica

Marilyn L. Barton: Senior Coordinator, Production Control
Steven Bosco: Director, Editorial Technologies
Lisa S. Braucher: Senior Producer and Data Editor
Yvette Charboneau: Senior Copy Editor
Kathy Nakamura: Manager, Media Acquisition

Rosen Educational Services
Heather M. Moore Niver: Editor
Nelson Sá: Art Director
Cindy Reiman: Photography Manager
Matthew Cauli: Designer, Cover Design
Introduction by Heather M. Moore Niver

Library of Congress Cataloging-in-Publication Data

The outer planets : Jupiter, Saturn, Uranus, and Neptune / edited by Sherman Hollar.
    p. cm. — (The solar system)
"In association with Britannica Educational Publishing, Rosen Educational Services."
Includes bibliographical references and index.
ISBN 978-1-61530-518-6 (library binding)
1. Outer planets--Juvenile literature. I. Hollar, Sherman.
QB659.O98 2012
523.46—dc22

2011001378

Manufactured in the United States of America

CONTENTS

The most distant and perhaps most intriguing planets in our solar system are known as the outer planets: Jupiter, Saturn, Uranus, and Neptune. Of these bodies, ancient astronomers could see only bright Jupiter and Saturn in the night sky. Thanks to deep-space probes and constantly improving Earth-based observational technology, scientists today are steadily unraveling mysteries about the planets, their moons, and their rings. This book takes you on a journey to the most remote planets in our solar system.

Our first destination is Jupiter, the largest planet in the solar system. It is so big that more than 1,300 Earths could fit inside it. It is the fifth planet from the Sun but bright enough that we can see its multicolored stripes with only a small telescope. Also visible is a red oval called the Great Red Spot, which is a storm in Jupiter's atmosphere that has been going on for more than 300 years. Jupiter's surface and interior are composed mainly of hydrogen and helium. The planet has 63 known moons and a narrow system of rings. Its orbit is elliptical (oval), and one orbit is equal to about 11.86 Earth years.

Next we encounter Saturn, the second-largest planet in our solar system. Saturn was the most distant planet ancient astronomers could see. Like Jupiter, Saturn has a gaseous surface, mainly made up of hydrogen, and is surrounded by an atmosphere with complex weather patterns. Interior hydrogen is a liquid, and the core is liquid metallic hydrogen. Saturn has a typical elliptical orbit pattern. Its magnificent rings consist largely of water ice and dust particles. Although the rings are thin, the diameter of the main rings extends for some 170,000 miles (270,000 kilometers), and the fainter outer rings extend even farther. Saturn also has more than 60 moons.

Uranus is the third-largest planet we encounter on our journey. It is seventh from the Sun. A small amount of methane in its atmosphere gives it a blue-green hue, but otherwise Uranus appears nearly featureless in visible light. Ancient astronomers could not see Uranus, and even 21st-century telescopes are not powerful enough to show great detail. Like all the planets, Uranus has an oval-shaped orbit, but its rotation is unusual. Instead of rotating almost perpendicular to its orbit like most planets, Uranus's rotation is nearly parallel to its orbit. Uranus has

Volcanoes erupt on Io, one of Jupiter's Galilean satellites, in a mosaic of images captured by the Galileo spacecraft. One plume visible on Io at the far left is about 90 miles (140 kilometers) high. Another plume at the center of the moon is revealed by its shadow, which extends to the right. **Photo NASA/JPL/Caltech (NASA photo # PIA01081)**

about a dozen narrow rings, which are not as bright as Saturn's, and 27 known moons. Like Jupiter and Saturn, this planet is not solid. It is made up of hydrogen, helium, water, and other compounds.

Finally, we arrive at the farthest planet from the Sun, Neptune. At more than 2.5 billion miles (4 billion kilometers) from Earth, Neptune was not discovered until the mid-1800s. Although Neptune is the smallest of the four outer planets, it is the densest. Neptune is a gas giant, too, and is primarily made up of hydrogen and some helium. Pressures in the planet's interior are likely high enough to render it liquid. Neptune spins so quickly that a day (one rotation) lasts only 16 hours. Neptune has a series of six rings, and four of the planet's 13 moons orbit within the rings. Curiously, one of Neptune's moons, Titron, revolves around the planet in a direction opposite the planet's rotation.

For many years Jupiter, Saturn, Uranus, and Neptune were shrouded in mystery. Astronomers have much to learn about this quartet of gas giants. Probes such as Voyager 1 and 2 have gathered enough data and photographs to present a broader picture of the planets, rings, and moons that you will learn about in these pages.

CHARACTERISTICS OF JUPITER

The fifth planet from the Sun and the solar system's largest planet by far is Jupiter. More than 1,300 Earths would fit inside it. The planet is one of the brightest objects in the night sky, and even a small telescope can reveal its multicolored stripes. These stripes are bands of clouds being pushed around the planet by strong east-west winds. Jupiter is a world of complex weather patterns. Its most prominent feature is an orange-red oval called the Great Red Spot. The oval is a storm system that has lasted at least 300 years and is bigger across than Earth and Mars combined.

Bands of pastel-colored clouds encircle the giant planet Jupiter, which appears in a composite of images taken by the Cassini spacecraft. The small black disk at lower left is a shadow cast by Jupiter's moon Europa. The enormous storm called the Great Red Spot is visible at lower right. The raw images were taken in two colors, which were processed to simulate Jupiter's natural colors. **NASA/JPL/University of Arizona**

Jupiter is not just bigger than Earth, it is also fundamentally different in composition. Jupiter has no solid surface. It is formed of the same elements, in roughly the same proportions, as the Sun and other stars. Like Saturn, it is made almost entirely of hydrogen and helium in liquid and gaseous forms. Although

A map shows the entire visible "surface" of Jupiter, including its bands of clouds, the Great Red Spot, and many smaller oval storms in the planet's massive atmosphere. The map is a cylindrical projection, like maps of Earth that show the planet stretched flat onto a rectangle. It was generated by computer from 36 images taken by the Cassini spacecraft and processed to simulate the planet's true colors. Jupiter's polar regions appear less clear because of the angle of the spacecraft's camera and because they were covered by a thicker haze. NASA/JPL/Space Science Institute

Jupiter is huge, it would have to be about 80 times more massive to generate nuclear reactions and become a star.

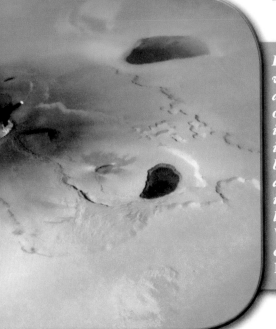

Hot, glowing lava erupts from a volcano on Jupiter's moon Io in an image captured by the Galileo orbiter. It is a mosaic of several images, including enhanced-color images taken in visible light. The bright white, yellow, and orange at left are false colors added to images taken at infrared wavelengths to indicate temperature. White is the hottest and orange the coolest. **NASA/JPL/California Institute of Technology**

Nevertheless, Jupiter reigns at the center of a system of dozens of moons like a miniature solar system. Four of the moons are quite large and would probably be considered planets themselves if they did not orbit a planet. They are remarkably dissimilar worlds. Io is the most volcanically active body in the solar system. Frequent eruptions renew its surface and cover over any craters that form. Europa's surface is also fairly young, but its features are smoothed not by fiery lava but by water ice, which possibly flows up from beneath the surface and freezes. Europa may harbor an ocean of warm, salty water just under its icy crust. Callisto has an ancient crater-scarred surface that seems to have been largely undisturbed by geologic activity for some 4 billion years. Ganymede, the solar system's largest moon, is bigger than the planet Mercury and has a planetlike magnetic field.

An outer planet, Jupiter is much farther from the Sun than Earth and the other inner planets are. Its orbit lies between the main asteroid belt and Saturn's orbit. Its inner planetary neighbor, Mars, orbits between the

Jupiter's Galilean moons—from left to right, Io, Europa, Ganymede, and Callisto—appear in a montage created with images from the Galileo orbiter. The images are scaled to show the moons' sizes relative to one another. **NASA/JPL/Caltech**

asteroid belt and Earth. Like the other outer planets—Saturn, Uranus, and Neptune—Jupiter is much larger and less dense than Earth and the other rocky inner planets.

SIZE, MASS, AND DENSITY

Jupiter is named for the ruler of the ancient Roman gods, the equivalent of the ancient Greek god Zeus. The ancient Romans did not know how large the planet is, but the name turned out to be fitting. Jupiter encompasses more matter than all the other planets in the solar system combined. Its diameter at the equator is some 88,846 miles (142,984 kilometers). It is about 320 times as massive as Earth. Jupiter's large mass produces strong gravitational effects on other members of the solar system. It forms gaps, for instance, in the distribution of the asteroids in the main belt and changes the trajectory of comets. The planet's density is very low, only about 1.3 times that of water. By comparison, Earth is more than 5.5 times denser than water.

ORBIT AND SPIN

Jupiter, like all the other planets, travels around the Sun in a slightly elliptical, or

oval-shaped, orbit. It completes one orbit in about 11.86 Earth years, which is the length of a year on Jupiter. Its average distance from the Sun is about 483 million miles (778 million kilometers), which is more than five times greater than Earth's.

Jupiter spins quite quickly on its axis, faster than the other seven planets. It completes one rotation in about 9 hours and 55 minutes, which is the length of a day on Jupiter. The atmosphere spins at slightly different rates, with the clouds near the equator completing a rotation a few minutes faster than the clouds at higher latitudes. The force of a planet's rotation causes it to bulge slightly at the equator and to flatten slightly at the poles. Jupiter's rapid spin accentuates this, so it is less perfectly spherical than most other planets. Jupiter's spin axis is tilted only about 3 degrees. For this reason, it does not have seasons like Earth, Mars, and other planets with tilted axes.

RING SYSTEM

Jupiter's thin ring system was discovered only by spacecraft, by Voyager 1 in 1979. The rings are composed of tiny dust particles that orbit the planet. The main ring is about 4,000

miles (6,400 kilometers) wide and 19 miles (30 kilometers) thick. Its outer edge lies some 80,000 miles (129,000 kilometers) from the planet's center. Straddling the main ring are an inner cloudlike ring of particles called the halo and two outer rings. The outer rings are called gossamer rings because the particles within them are quite thinly distributed. All the rings are formed of debris produced

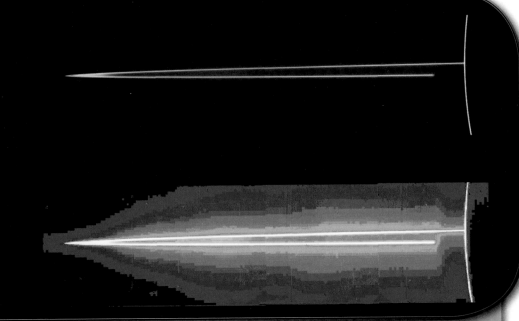

Two images taken by the Galileo orbiter show the thin main ring of Jupiter nearly edge-on. The top image shows the ring of particles in scattered natural light. In the bottom image, colors added in processing highlight the extremely faint mist of particles extending above and below the ring. The nearer arm of the ring in each image disappears close to Jupiter where it passes into the planet's shadow. **NASA/JPL**

when small fragments of asteroids, comets, and other objects collide with Jupiter's four small inner moons. The main ring seems to be formed of debris from the moons Metis and Adrastea. The gossamer rings are fed by Amalthea and Thebe.

MOONS

Jupiter has 63 known moons, and more are likely still to be discovered. The four biggest moons are each about the size of Earth's Moon or larger. In order of increasing distance from Jupiter, they are Io, Europa, Ganymede, and Callisto. They were the first objects in the solar system to be discovered with a telescope, by Galileo in 1610. They are now called the Galilean satellites in his honor. Amalthea was the next of Jupiter's moons to be discovered. It was first observed by Edward Emerson Barnard in 1892 through a telescope. All the other moons of Jupiter were discovered by examining images captured by Earth-based telescopes or the Voyager spacecraft. Many of the planet's smaller moons are less than 5 miles (8 kilometers) in diameter and were discovered in 2000 or later, with powerful telescopes and highly sensitive electronic imaging equipment.

A small, elaborately patterned area of Europa's ice crust appears in an enhanced-color image that combines images and data gathered by the Galileo spacecraft. Observations of such intricate structures on Europa indicate that in the recent past its crust cracked and huge blocks of ice rotated slightly before being refrozen in new positions. The size and geometry of the blocks suggest that their motion was enabled by an underlying layer of icy slush or liquid water present at the time of the disruption. **NASA/JPL/California Institute of Technology**

Jupiter's eight inner moons—the four small moons Metis, Adrastea, Amalthea, and Thebe plus the four Galilean satellites— orbit the planet in fairly circular paths. The plane of their orbit is also nearly the same as the plane in which Jupiter orbits the Sun. For these two reasons, the moons are called regular. The rest of Jupiter's moons are irregular. That is, they have a particularly elongated or tilted orbit, or both. Also, the regular moons

GALILEO

Modern physics owes its beginning to Galileo, who was the first astronomer to use a telescope. By discovering four satellites of the planet Jupiter, he gave visual evidence that supported the Copernican theory. Galileo thus helped disprove much of the medieval thinking in science.

In 1592 the University of Padua offered Galileo a professorship in mathematics. About 1609, after word from Holland of Hans Lippershey's newly invented telescope reached him, he built his own version of the instrument. He developed magnifying power until on Jan. 7, 1610, he saw four satellites of Jupiter. He also saw the mountains and craters on the moon and found the Milky Way to be a dense collection of stars. Galileo moved to Florence in September 1610 and was a philosopher and mathematician there for many years. In 1609 Johannes Kepler published his laws of planetary motion based on the Copernican theory. Galileo strongly supported this view. In 1616 he received a formal warning that the theory was contrary to the teachings of the church. Nevertheless, he again supported the Copernican view in a dialogue, *The Great Systems of the Universe*.

During his last eight years, Galileo lived near Florence under house arrest for having "held and taught" Copernican doctrine. He became blind in 1637 but continued to work until his death on Jan. 8, 1642. Nearly 342 years later, Galileo was pardoned by Pope John Paul II and the Roman Catholic Church finally accepted his teachings.

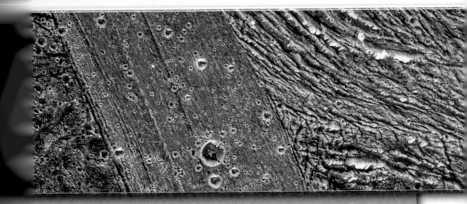

...nymede's surface taken by the Galileo spacecraft shows ...erse terrain about 55 miles (90 kilometers) long. The ...band cutting through the center is the youngest ter-...the oldest terrain in the area, at right, from a grooved, ...' terrain that is intermediate in age, at left. **NASA/JPL/ ...tue of Technology**

orbit Jupiter in the same direction as the planet's rotation, while most of the irregular moons orbit in the opposite direction. Scientists believe that Jupiter's eight regular moons probably formed along with Jupiter some 4.6 billion years ago. As Jupiter formed from a disk of gas and dust surrounding the Sun, its regular moons formed from such a disk surrounding the planet. The irregular moons may have been asteroids, comets, or fragments that passed close enough to Jupiter for its gravity to capture them into orbits.

The two inner Galilean satellites, Io and Europa, are much denser than the outer two, Ganymede and Callisto. Io and Europa are

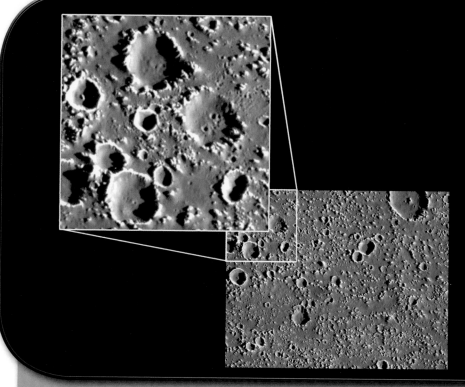

A heavily cratered and pitted region of Callisto's ancient surface appears in an image (bottom right) *taken by the Galileo spacecraft and an enlargement* (upper left) *to show detail. The region shown in the bottom image is about 45 miles (72 kilometers) across.* **NASA/JPL/Space Science Institute**

probably rocky bodies with compositions roughly similar to Earth's Moon. Ganymede and Callisto are probably roughly half rock and half water ice or some other substance of low density. The surfaces of three of the moons, Europa, Ganymede, and Callisto, are icy.

PHYSICAL FEATURES AND EXPLORATION OF JUPITER

Although even a modest telescope can show much detail on Jupiter, much was unknown about the planet until relatively recently. The first three spacecraft missions to Jupiter—named Pioneer, Voyager, and Galileo—dramatically increased scientists' knowledge about the giant planet in the late 20th century.

ATMOSPHERE

Jupiter has a massive atmosphere, or layer of surrounding gases. It is about 86 percent hydrogen and 14 percent helium by mass. The Sun has a similar composition, at about 71 percent hydrogen and 28 percent helium by mass. Planetary scientists believe that the four outer planets all received about the same proportions of hydrogen and helium as the Sun when the solar system formed from a disk of gas and dust. It is thought that in Jupiter and Saturn more of the helium is concentrated in the interior. Jupiter's atmosphere also contains trace amounts of many other gases, including methane, ammonia,

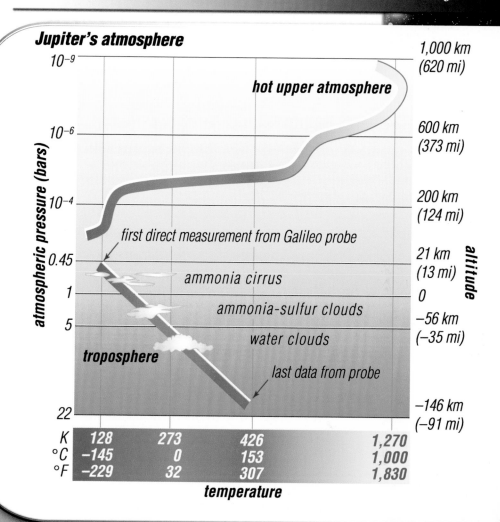

Jupiter's atmosphere

hot upper atmosphere

first direct measurement from Galileo probe

ammonia cirrus

ammonia-sulfur clouds

water clouds

troposphere

last data from probe

atmospheric pressure (bars)

10^{-9}
10^{-6}
10^{-4}
0.45
1
5
22

altitude

1,000 km (620 mi)
600 km (373 mi)
200 km (124 mi)
21 km (13 mi)
0
−56 km (−35 mi)
−146 km (−91 mi)

K	128	273	426	1,270
°C	−145	0	153	1,000
°F	−229	32	307	1,830

temperature

A graph shows the temperatures and pressures at different levels of Jupiter's atmosphere, The graph shows altitudes from 1,000 kilometers (620 miles) above the reference level to 146 kilometers (91 miles) below it. Pictures of clouds indicate the approximate positions of the expected cloud layers. The probe did not detect clouds, having descended in a nearly cloudless spot. Some temperatures and pressures were directly measured by the probe, while others were deduced from other data collected by it. Encyclopædia Britannica, Inc.

water vapor, hydrogen sulfide, and hydrogen deuteride.

In the lower parts of the atmosphere, where clouds form, it generally gets colder with increasing height above the planet. At higher levels, the gases and particles absorb solar radiation. This makes the middle and upper levels of the atmosphere hotter, with temperatures increasing with altitude.

The clouds in Jupiter's atmosphere appear as alternating dark and bright bands roughly parallel to the equator. The darker bands are called belts, while the brighter bands are called zones. The clouds are also separated into different layers by depth. They range in color from white to tawny yellow, brown, salmon, and blue-gray. Scientists think that the clouds vary in color because they contain different chemicals.

The highest clouds are white and are composed of frozen crystals of ammonia. The temperature at their tops is about -240 °F (-150 °C). Clouds in the main deck are tawny colored and lower in the atmosphere, where the temperature is about -100 °F (-70 °C). In some places holes in the layers of tawny clouds reveal dark brown clouds below. The tawny and brown clouds are probably made mostly of ammonium hydrosulfide, and their colors may result from other sulfur compounds. Scientists also think there is a lower deck of clouds formed of water ice and water droplets. Blue-gray and purplish areas are found only near the equator. They are thought to be areas with relatively few or no clouds.

Jupiter has a turbulent atmosphere, and its cloud systems form and change in a matter of hours or days. However, the underlying pattern of wind currents has been stable over decades. Strong winds blow east or west through the atmosphere in several alternating bands. They are interrupted in places by large whirling storm systems that appear from above as ovals.

The Great Red Spot projects higher than the planet's highest white clouds, and it probably also descends well below the main cloud layers. There is no clear evidence that the storm causes upwelling of material

As of 2006, Jupiter had two large red spots. The Great Red Spot, below the equator at right, and the much younger red storm nicknamed Red Spot, Jr., at lower center, appear in a false-color image taken by the Hubble Space Telescope in April 2006. The smaller red spot is about as big across as Earth. The image was taken in visible light and at near-infrared wavelengths. NASA/ESA

JUPITER'S GREAT RED SPOT

The most persistent feature in Jupiter's atmosphere is the famous Great Red Spot. It has been observed from Earth since 1664. The spot is a huge oval-shaped storm system in the planet's southern hemisphere, with strong winds swirling counterclockwise about a high-pressure center. In other words, it is like an anti-cyclone on Earth. It covers an area larger than Earth itself, however, with dimensions of about 12,400 by 7,500 miles (20,000 by 12,000 kilometers). Material within the spot completes one circle about every seven days. This means that winds around the outer parts of the storm probably reach super-hurricane force, blowing at some 250 miles (400 kilometers) per hour. As Jupiter rotates, the storm system moves in longitude with respect to the clouds, but it remains centered at about latitude 22° S.

Ribbons of clouds wind through the area around Jupiter's huge Great Red Spot, a whirling storm system, in an image captured by Voyager 1. Below the Great Red Spot is another large whirling storm, which appears as a white oval. **NASA/JPL**

at its center, though some vertical movement would be expected. Scientists are uncertain why the spot is reddish. They think its color might result from complex organic molecules, red phosphorous, or sulfur compounds. Any of these materials could be produced by lightning. They also could result from material upwelling to high altitudes, where it reacts chemically with ultraviolet radiation from the Sun.

Three smaller, white, oval-shaped storms were observed just south of the Great Red Spot starting in about the 1940s. The three ovals merged in 1998–2000, creating a single storm system nearly half as big across as the Great Red Spot. Scientists believe that a similar merger may have created the Great Red Spot. In fact, in 2006 the merged storm (Red Spot, Jr.) turned the same salmon-red as the larger spot, for unknown reasons. Another smaller oval storm turned reddish in 2008, but later in the year this third red spot collided with the Great Red Spot. The collision deformed the smaller storm and turned it pale again.

INTERIOR

The atmosphere surrounding Jupiter makes up only a small percentage of the planet. Scientists cannot directly observe the planet below the atmosphere, however. Instead, they form theoretical models based on many known properties such as the planet's size, mass, density, rotation rate, heat balance, and atmospheric pressures and temperatures.

Like the atmosphere, the interior is composed mainly of hydrogen and helium. Inside the planet, pressures and temperatures increase greatly with depth, so the hydrogen and helium get denser and denser. Starting at about a quarter of the way down to the center, the pressure has probably squeezed the hydrogen into liquid metallic form. In this state, the electrons are stripped away from the atomic nuclei, so the fluid hydrogen would conduct electricity like a metal.

At Jupiter's center is probably a very dense core. Different models have the core about a third as big as Earth to a bit bigger than Earth. Temperatures there may reach nearly 45,000 °F (25,000 °C). The pressure in the core is likely 50 million to 100 million times the pressure at sea level on Earth.

Jupiter has some sort of internal heat source. The planet emits nearly twice as much energy as it receives from the Sun, for reasons that are not entirely clear. Much of this heat was probably acquired during the planet's formation some 4.6 billion years ago. As

the planet continues to cool off, it gradually emits heat. Scientists think that another process probably also generates some of the heat. This process involves helium separating out into droplets and sinking toward the planet's center. The friction of the helium droplets pushing against the liquid metallic hydrogen would convert some energy to heat.

MAGNETIC FIELD AND MAGNETOSPHERE

Jupiter has the largest and strongest magnetic field of all the planets. The planet's rapidly rotating, electrically conducting interior is thought to give rise to the strong field. Like Earth's magnetic field, it has two poles, north and south, like a giant bar magnet. The orientation of the poles is opposite that of Earth, so that a compass would point south on Jupiter. Jupiter's magnetic field is also tilted about 10 degrees relative to its spin axis.

The region of space dominated by Jupiter's magnetic field is called its magnetosphere. It is a huge teardrop-shaped area. On the side nearest the Sun it extends about 1.9 million miles (3 million kilometers). On that side, the magnetosphere holds off the solar wind, which is a flow of electrically charged particles from the Sun. This creates a large shock wave. On the opposite side of Jupiter, the solar wind pushes the magnetosphere's tail out to the orbit of Saturn, some 400 million miles (650 million kilometers) away.

Jupiter's magnetic field traps electrically charged particles around the planet. The particles move around Jupiter in roughly doughnut-shaped regions. Electrons traveling almost at the speed of light radiate energy as they spiral through the regions. These regions of intense radiation are similar to but stronger than Earth's Van Allen radiation belts.

Jupiter strongly emits radio waves in both intermittent bursts at longer wavelengths and steady streams at shorter wavelengths. Both types result from charged particles moving in the planet's magnetosphere. The bursts are sometimes the most intense source of radio "noise" in the sky. They were first detected in the 1950s, and they provided the first clues that Jupiter had a magnetic field. The steady emissions, which were discovered later, are radiated by the charged particles trapped in the radiation belts. This stream of radio waves varies somewhat in intensity and orientation as the planet rotates. The variations have a char-acteristic period, which is the rotation rate of Jupiter's magnetic field. The rotation rate of

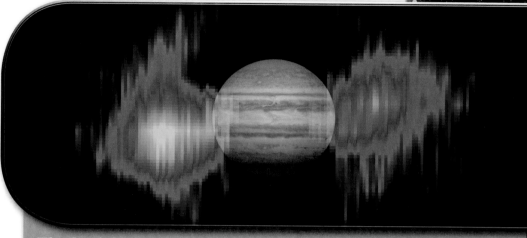

The Cassini spacecraft mapped Jupiter's radiation belts by measuring the strength of their radio emissions at a frequency of 13,800 megahertz (13.8 billion cycles per second). Color coding indicates the strength of the emission, with yellows and reds being the most intense. A photograph of Jupiter taken by telescope has been added to show the size and orientation of the belts relative to the planet. **NASA/JPL**

the magnetic field is also the rotation rate of the planet's interior, which produces the field.

The bursts of radio waves come from three distinct areas around Jupiter. The position of the moon Io as it orbits Jupiter is thought to strongly influence these bursts. Magnetic field lines connect Jupiter to Io. They enclose a doughnut-shaped region of space called a flux tube between the planet and the moon. This flux tube moves along with Io. In addition, volcanic eruptions on Io release a cloud of electrically charged particles that accompanies Io along its orbit. As the cloud passes through

Jupiter's magnetic field, an electric current of some 5 million amperes is generated. Scientists believe that the radio bursts are probably emitted by electrons that spiral along the magnetic field lines in the flux tube connecting Io and Jupiter.

Auroras similar to Earth's northern and southern lights appear at times near Jupiter's poles. As on Earth, the auroras result from charged particles in the radiation belts crashing into molecules of the upper atmosphere.

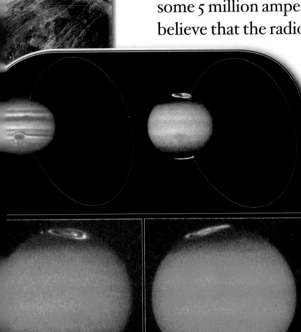

Auroras light up Jupiter's poles in images taken by the Hubble Space Telescope. The two lower images are in false color and were taken in ultraviolet light. They follow changes in the brightness and structure of the auroras as the planet rotates. In the two top images, a line was added to trace the path of the magnetic flux tube, or current of charged particles, that links Jupiter and its moon Io. The image at top left was taken in visible light, while the one at top right was taken in ultraviolet light. AURA/STScI/NASA/JPL

SPACECRAFT EXPLORATION

Two Pioneer spacecraft flew by Jupiter in the early 1970s to survey the planet's basic environment and assess whether its radiation levels would permit future spacecraft exploration.

They were launched by the U.S. National Aeronautics and Space Administration (NASA). Pioneer 10 was the first spacecraft to travel beyond the asteroid belt to the outer part of the solar system. Flying within 80,000 miles (130,000 kilometers) of Jupiter's cloud tops in December 1973, it transmitted the first close-up images of the planet. It also discovered the huge "tail" of the planet's magnetosphere. Pioneer 11 followed, passing within about 27,000 miles (43,000 kilometers) of the cloud tops in December 1974.

NASA's Voyagers 1 and 2 flew past Jupiter in March and July of 1979, respectively. Their instrumentation was more robust and sophisticated than the Pioneers', and they gathered much valuable data. Close-up images from the spacecraft also uncovered a few new moons, volcanic activity on Io, and a thin ring around Jupiter.

In October 1989 NASA launched the Galileo spacecraft toward Jupiter for an extended study of the planet, its moons, and its magnetic field. When it reached the planet in July 1995, it released a probe, which became the first human-made object to make contact with an outer planet, in December 1995. The probe parachuted through about 100 miles (165 kilometers) of the atmosphere,

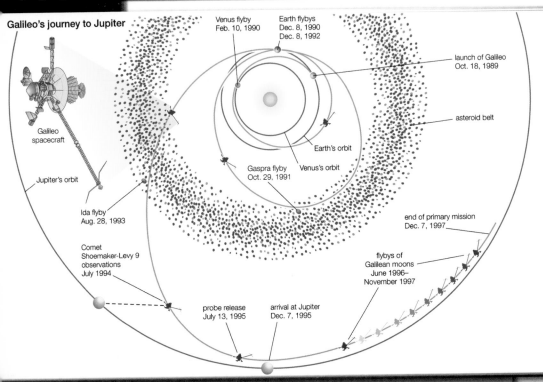

Galileo's journey to Jupiter

Venus flyby
Feb. 10, 1990

Earth flybys
Dec. 8, 1990
Dec. 8, 1992

launch of Galileo
Oct. 18, 1989

asteroid belt

Galileo
spacecraft

Earth's orbit

Jupiter's orbit

Gaspra flyby
Oct. 29, 1991

Venus's orbit

Ida flyby
Aug. 28, 1993

end of primary mission
Dec. 7, 1997

Comet
Shoemaker-Levy 9
observations
July 1994

flybys of
Galilean moons
June 1996–
November 1997

probe release
July 13, 1995

arrival at Jupiter
Dec. 7, 1995

Artwork depicts the journey of the Galileo spacecraft to Jupiter. Galileo's multiple gravity-assist trajectory involved three planetary flybys (Venus once and Earth twice), two passes into the asteroid belt, and a fortuitous view of the collision of Comet Shoemaker-Levy 9 with Jupiter. Encyclopædia Britannica, Inc.

relaying measurements of the chemical composition, temperature, and pressure before being destroyed within about an hour by the planet's extreme conditions. Scientists expected the Galileo probe to detect water clouds below the main cloud deck, but it did not. Unfortunately, the probe seems to have dropped through a nearly cloudless area of the atmosphere.

The Galileo atmospheric probe (shown before its launch) became the first human-made object to make contact with one of the outer planets. In 1995 the Galileo orbiter released the 747-pound (339-kilogram) probe on a course toward Jupiter. With the aid of a parachute, the probe slowly descended through the giant planet's atmosphere, using its six science instruments to measure such properties as temperature, pressure, density, cloud structure, and chemical composition. **NASA/Ames Research Center**

The Galileo orbiter transmitted spectacular images and a wealth of data about Jupiter and its four largest moons. The orbiter completed its original mission in 1997. Because it was still performing well, NASA extended its mission three times, until the craft was nearly out of propellant. In September 2003 NASA intentionally sent it on a collision course with Jupiter's atmosphere, which destroyed the craft.

A different opportunity to study Jupiter arose in 1994, when pieces of Comet Shoemaker-Levy 9's nucleus crashed into the

Several enormous, dark scars temporarily formed in Jupiter's atmosphere when pieces of Comet Shoemaker-Levy 9 collided with it in 1994. The image was made by the Hubble Space Telescope on July 22, the last day of the impacts. NASA/Hubble Space Telescope Comet Team

planet's atmosphere. Scientists observed the effects of the explosions from Earth-based and Earth-orbiting telescopes and through images captured by the Galileo spacecraft. The impacts and the temporary black scars they formed in the planet's clouds provided clues about the composition and structure of Jupiter's atmosphere as well as about the comet's consistency.

Additional data and images of Jupiter were captured by NASA's Cassini spacecraft as it flew by the planet in 2000–01 on its way to Saturn. Among the phenomena studied through Cassini were large amounts of charged particles escaping from one side of Jupiter's magnetosphere.

CHARACTERISTICS OF SATURN

The sixth planet from the Sun is Saturn. Dusty chunks of ice—some the size of a house, others of a grain of sand—make up its extraordinary rings. The other outer planets also have rings, but Saturn's are much larger and more complex. The planet is a popular target for amateur astronomers because even a small telescope can reveal the dazzling rings. To the unaided eye, Saturn looks like a bright nontwinkling point of light. It was the most distant planet known to ancient astronomers.

Saturn was named after the ancient Roman god of agriculture. His counterpart in ancient Greek mythology was Cronus, the father of Zeus (the counterpart of the Roman god Jupiter). The planet Jupiter is Saturn's nearest neighbor and the closest to it in size and composition. Like Jupiter, Saturn is a giant world formed mainly of hydrogen with no solid surface. It has a massive atmosphere, or surrounding layer of gases, with complex weather patterns. Saturn's orbit lies between those of Jupiter and Uranus.

Saturn's extensive system of icy moons includes nine major moons and dozens of

The planet Saturn and its spectacular rings appear in a natural-color composite of 126 images taken by the Cassini spacecraft. The view is directed toward Saturn's southern hemisphere, which is tipped toward the Sun. Shadows cast by the rings are visible against the bluish northern hemisphere, while the planet's shadow appears on the rings to the left. NASA/JPL/Space Science Institute

small ones. Some moons help create the rings and maintain their shape. Titan, the largest of Saturn's moons, is bigger than the planet Mercury. It is the only moon in the solar system known to have a dense atmosphere.

SIZE, MASS, AND DENSITY

Saturn is the solar system's second largest and second most massive planet, after Jupiter. The diameter at its equator is about 74,898 miles (120,536 kilometers). Because the planet has no solid surface, its diameter is measured at a level where the atmospheric pressure is 1 bar, which is equal to the pressure at sea level on Earth. Saturn's diameter is more than nine times larger than Earth's. The planet is about 95 times as massive as Earth and has more than 750 times its volume. By comparison, Jupiter is about 1.2 times as big as Saturn and 3.2 times as massive.

Saturn has the lowest mean density of any of the planets. With only about 70 percent the density of water on average, the planet would float if it could be placed in water. Earth's density, however, is about 550 percent that of water, and Jupiter's is about 130 percent.

ORBIT AND SPIN

Saturn revolves around the Sun in a slightly elliptical, or oval-shaped, orbit at a mean distance of about 887 million miles (1.427 billion kilometers). Its orbit is about 9.5 times farther out than Earth's. The closest Earth and Saturn ever get to each other is about 746 million miles

The Huygens probe captured the first close-up photographs of the surface of Saturn's moon Titan. The stones strewn over the moon's extraordinarily cold surface may be water ice frozen to the point that it acts mechanically like rock. **ESA/NASA/JPL/University of Arizona**

(1.2 billion kilometers). It takes Saturn some 29.4 Earth years to complete one revolution around the Sun, so a year on Saturn is about 29.4 times longer than a year on Earth.

Because Saturn is not solid, it has no single rotation rate. However, all parts of the planet spin quickly. Clouds in the atmosphere near the equator swirl around fastest, taking about 10 hours, 10 minutes for each rotation. It takes the planet's deep interior roughly 30–40 minutes longer to complete each rotation. A day on a planet is defined by its rotation period, so a day on Saturn is about 10.8 Earth hours, or less than half as long as a day on Earth.

As in other planets, the force of the rotation causes some bulging at the equator and flattening at the poles. Saturn's rapid rotation and low average density make it the least spherical of all the planets. The diameter at its poles is about 10 percent smaller than the diameter at its equator. Jupiter actually spins a bit faster than Saturn, but its shape is less distorted. Jupiter's greater density helps it better resist the force produced by the rapid rotation.

Saturn's rotational axis is tilted about 26.7 degrees relative to the ecliptic, which is an imaginary plane passing through the Sun and Earth's orbit. As Saturn orbits the Sun, first one hemisphere and then the other is tipped closer to the Sun. As a result, Saturn experiences seasons like Earth, which is tilted about 23.5 degrees on its axis. Because each trip around the Sun takes longer for Saturn than Earth, its seasons are longer. Each season on Saturn lasts more than seven years.

The tilt of Saturn's axis also displays the rings at different angles to observers on Earth. The rings are thin and flat and always lie in the same plane as the planet's equator. As Earth and Saturn travel around the Sun, Saturn and its rings are more or less tilted toward observers on Earth. At most, they are tilted about 30 degrees. The view varies over about a 30-year period, the time it takes Saturn to complete one orbit. Viewers on Earth see the sunlit northern side of the rings for about 15 years, and then the sunlit southern side for about the next 15 years. The rings are practically invisible when their thin edge is pointed directly at

Saturn and its rings are tilted at varying angles toward Earth as the two planets orbit the Sun. Five images taken at about one-year intervals by the Hubble Space Telescope show the change in ring orientation from 1996 to 2000. In the first image, at the bottom, the rings appear nearly edge-on, while in the last image, at the top, the rings are opened to nearly their widest angle as seen from Earth's vicinity. NASA and The Hubble Heritage Team (STScI/AURA) Acknowledgment: R. G. French (Wellesley College), J. Cuzzi (NASA/Ames), L. Dones (SwRI), and J. Lissauer (NASA/Ames)

Earth, which happens for short periods when Earth crosses the plane of the rings.

RING SYSTEM

Saturn's spectacular rings have long been admired for their beauty. Its prominent rings are brighter and broader than the faint, narrow principal rings of the other outer planets. They are the easiest rings to see from Earth and so were the first to be discovered. Galileo observed them through an early telescope in 1610, but he did not identify them as rings. In 1655, using a more powerful telescope, the scientist Christiaan Huygens was able to see a flat, apparently solid ring around Saturn. The scientist James Clerk Maxwell demonstrated mathematically in 1857 that the rings could not be solid but must be composed of many small particles. This theory was confirmed by observations made by James Keeler in the 1890s. In the 1980s the cameras of the Voyager spacecraft revealed that there are really hundreds of thousands of individual rings (or "ringlets") around Saturn. The Cassini spacecraft discovered additional rings and structures within them in the 2000s.

The main rings have a diameter of about 170,000 miles (270,000 kilometers), and the

Saturn's three main rings appear in a natural-color composite of six images taken by the Cassini spacecraft. The view is from below the ring plane, with the rings tilted at an angle of about 4°. The major gaps in the rings are labeled. The distances are given in thousands of kilometers from the center of Saturn (1,000 kilometers equals about 621 miles) and in Saturn radii (the planet's radius is about 60,268 kilometers, or 37,449 miles). Encyclopædia Britannica, Inc.

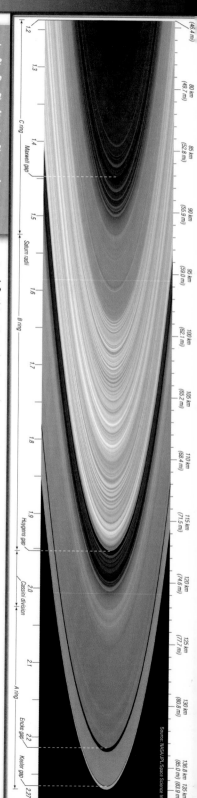

fainter outer rings extend much farther. The rings are quite thin, however, reaching a maximum thickness of roughly 300 feet (100 meters). They are made of countless particles, largely of water ice and dust, all orbiting Saturn like tiny moons. The particles range in size from no bigger than a speck of dust to the size of cars or houses. There are many more small particles than large ones. The individual particles that make up the rings have not been seen directly. However, scientists can determine their size distribution and composition by the way different parts of the rings reflect light, radio signals, and other radiation.

The rings occur in groups. The three main groups, from farthest to closest to Saturn, are called the A ring, the B ring, and the C ring. These three rings are visible

43

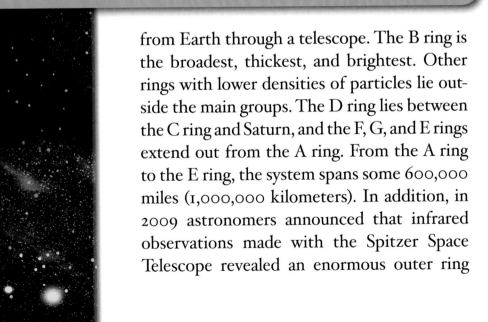

A dramatic backlit view of Saturn reveals its ring system as never before seen. From the vicinity of Earth, the planet and its rings always appear nearly fully illuminated. This backlit view is a mosaic of many images captured by the Cassini spacecraft while flying in Saturn's shadow, with the Sun on the opposite side of the planet. The colors have been exaggerated to bring out greater detail. From the planet's nightside, the rings appear bright, and light reflected off the rings partly illuminates Saturn itself. Easily visible surrounding the stunning main rings are the narrow G ring and the diffuse E ring. **NASA/JPL/Space Science Institute**

from Earth through a telescope. The B ring is the broadest, thickest, and brightest. Other rings with lower densities of particles lie outside the main groups. The D ring lies between the C ring and Saturn, and the F, G, and E rings extend out from the A ring. From the A ring to the E ring, the system spans some 600,000 miles (1,000,000 kilometers). In addition, in 2009 astronomers announced that infrared observations made with the Spitzer Space Telescope revealed an enormous outer ring that begins a few million miles beyond the E ring and extends another few million miles outward. The particles that make up this ring are sparsely distributed.

Many gaps occur between the rings. The gaps are regions where far fewer particles are found. Some of the major gaps are named after astronomers who studied Saturn. The main gap between the A and B rings is called the Cassini division. It was named after the astronomer Gian Domenico Cassini, who discovered the gap in 1675.

Moons

At least 60 moons orbit Saturn, in addition to the chunks of material in the rings. Nine of them have diameters greater than 125 miles (200 kilometers). In order of distance from Saturn, these major moons are Mimas, Enceladus, Tethys, Dione, Rhea, Titan, Hyperion, Iapetus, and Phoebe. All of them were discovered before the 20th century. The rest of Saturn's moons were discovered in the late 20th or early 21st centuries, in images captured by spacecraft or by powerful Earth-based telescopes equipped with particularly sensitive electronic detectors. Many of those moons are quite small.

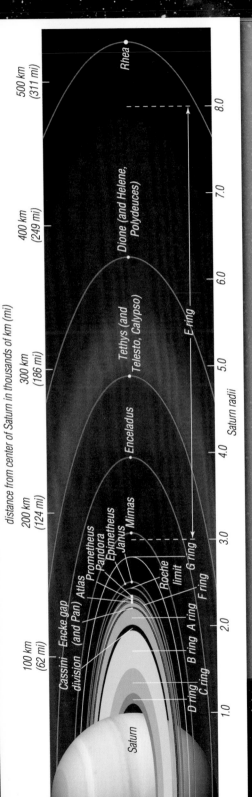

distance from center of Saturn in thousands of km (mi)

500 km (311 mi)

400 km (249 mi)

300 km (186 mi)

200 km (124 mi)

100 km (62 mi)

Rhea

Dione (and Helene, Polydeuces)

Tethys (and Telesto, Calypso)

E ring

Enceladus

Prometheus
Pandora
Epimetheus
Janus
Mimas

Atlas

Encke gap (and Pan)

Cassini division

Roche limit

G ring

F ring

B ring A ring

D ring

C ring

Saturn

Saturn radii

8.0
7.0
6.0
5.0
4.0
3.0
2.0
1.0

How Saturn's Rings and Moons Interact

Saturn's rings have a complex structure, and they interact with many of the planet's moons in many ways. The outermost rings seem to consist of small particles that are continually shed by moons. The Cassini spacecraft revealed that erupting geysers of water vapor and water ice on the moon Enceladus feed particles into the E ring. In addition, moons send particles into the outer rings when objects collide with them. In fact, Saturn's main rings may have been formed by an icy moon or moons that completely broke apart, perhaps tens of millions of years ago.

Many of Saturn's moons orbit the planet from within the extensive ring system. The red lines in the diagram indicate the orbits of some of these moons. The distances are given in thousands of kilometers from the center of Saturn (1,000 kilometers equals about 621 miles) and in Saturn radii (the planet's radius is about 60,268 kilometers, or 37,450 miles). **Encyclopædia Britannica, Inc.**

The diffuse particles of the enormous outermost ring probably come from the moon Phoebe.

Several small inner moons orbit Saturn embedded within the ring system. As these moons and others orbit the planet, their gravity affects the distribution of the ring particles. For instance, the moon Pan acts as a "sweeper," clearing particles from its orbital vicinity. This creates a gap in the rings called the Encke gap. Other moons act as "shepherds," by helping to keep the ring material in place. The shepherd moons Pandora and Prometheus orbit on either side of the F ring and constrain its particles into a narrow band. Their gravity is thought to be responsible for that ring's braided and knotted appearance.

Saturn's inner moons are called regular because they orbit in nearly circular paths in or near the plane of Saturn's orbit. The inner moons include all of Saturn's major moons except Phoebe, plus about a dozen others. The planet's outer moons are irregular, having highly elongated or tilted orbits, or both. The eight large inner moons are thought to have formed along with Saturn about 4.6 billion years ago. The outer moons probably started out as other objects but came too close to Saturn and were captured by its gravity.

The planet's largest moon, Titan, is remarkable in several ways. Its diameter is

The Cassini spacecraft photographed Dione, one of Saturn's major moons, majestically orbiting just above the planet's thin rings, which are seen edge-on. Saturn itself is at back. The curving bands across the planet's cloud tops are shadows cast by the rings. **NASA/JPL/Space Science Institute**

some 3,200 miles (5,150 kilometers), making it the second largest moon in the solar system. Only Jupiter's moon Ganymede is bigger. Unique among all moons, Titan has clouds and a very dense atmosphere. The atmosphere is even denser than Earth's, with a surface pressure that is about 1.5 times greater. Like Earth, Titan has an atmosphere that is mostly nitrogen. Titan's atmosphere also has about 5 percent methane and trace amounts of other gases. Methane might play a role in its atmosphere similar to that of water vapor on Earth. Liquid methane probably rains out of the clouds.

Titan itself is thought to be about half rock and half ices (mostly water ice mixed with some frozen ammonia and methane). It is about 1.9 times as dense as water. The temperature just above the surface is only about -290 °F (-179 °C).

A thick, orangish haze envelops the moon, so little was known about its surface features until the Cassini-Huygens mission arrived. It discovered that the surface is fairly young and sculpted by the wind. What seem to be vast sand dunes appear in radar images of areas near the equator. Scientists expected to find large oceans of liquid methane, but none were found. However, radar images taken by Cassini show many patches in the polar regions that are probably lake beds—some dry and some apparently filled with liquid, likely methane or ethane. In addition, dark channels, perhaps carved by methane rain, are common on Titan's surface. Some channels have extensive systems of tributaries.

The planet's other major moons are much smaller. They have low average densities and mostly bright, reflective surfaces that are rich in ices, mostly water ice. Their surfaces are so cold that the ice behaves like rock and can retain craters, which are the scars of collisions with other objects.

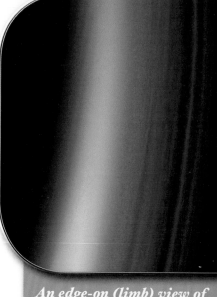

An edge-on (limb) view of the atmosphere of Titan, Saturn's largest moon, reveals many fine layers of haze. Titan is the only moon known to have a dense atmosphere. The image was taken in ultraviolet light by the Cassini spacecraft and was processed to simulate natural colors. **NASA/JPL/Space Science Institute**

In general, the more craters a solid body has, the older its surface. Mimas, Tethys, Dione, Rhea, Hyperion, Iapetus, and Phoebe are all heavily cratered. Mimas has one crater that is about a third as big across as Mimas itself. It is one of the largest-known craters in the solar system in relation to the size of the object. Though largely crater-scarred, Dione and Rhea also have smoother plains and other features that suggest their interiors may have been geologically active more recently. Parts of their icy surfaces seem to have melted and refrozen at some point.

Portions of Enceladus are geologically active today. It is Saturn's brightest moon, with a surface of almost pure water ice. A hot spot near its south pole fuels geysers that spew large amounts of water vapor and water ice. The water ice particles from these eruptions form Saturn's E ring. The surface of Enceladus has few large

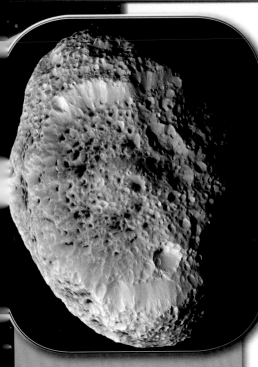

The crater-scarred surface of Hyperion, a major moon of Saturn, appears in an image taken by the Cassini spacecraft. Hyperion's interior may be a loose collection of ice blocks interspersed with holes, which would account for its low mean density (half that of water ice) and would explain its unusual "spongy" appearance. **NASA/ JPL/Space Science Institute**

The icy surface of Saturn's moon Enceladus reflects more light than newly fallen snow. A false-color mosaic of images from the Cassini spacecraft shows the unusual fractures dubbed "tiger stripes" in blue. The tiger stripes are found in the south polar region, where plumes of water vapor and ice particles erupt. **NASA/JPL/Space Science Institute**

craters overall and some crater-free areas that must have formed fairly recently. This suggests that it may have been internally active recently in other areas besides the south.

PHYSICAL FEATURES AND EXPLORATION OF SATURN

The physical features of Saturn continue to fascinate astronomers, and exciting new discoveries about the planet have been made possible by spacecraft exploration. To date, four unmanned spacecraft have visited Saturn, obtaining images and data that have greatly increased knowledge about the planet. The first three—Pioneer 11 and Voyagers 1 and 2—were flybys in the late 1970s and early 1980s. The Cassini-Huygens mission arrived in 2004 for a longer study of the planet and its moons and rings.

ATMOSPHERE

Saturn has an enormous atmosphere. It is made mostly of hydrogen, with some helium and smaller amounts of methane, ammonia, and other gases. Scientists think that small amounts of water vapor and hydrogen sulfide are probably found at lower levels of the atmosphere.

Saturn's composition, like Jupiter's, is quite similar to that of the Sun and other stars. Data from the Voyager mission suggest that Saturn's

atmosphere is about 91 percent hydrogen and 6 percent helium by mass, making it the most hydrogen-rich atmosphere in the solar system. In comparison, hydrogen makes up about 86 percent of Jupiter's atmosphere and about 71 percent of the Sun. Saturn's overall composition may be more similar to that of Jupiter and the Sun, but more of Saturn's helium may have settled into its interior. Also, some research suggests that the Voyager analysis underestimated the percentage of helium and overestimated the hydrogen.

In spacecraft images of Saturn, the surface one sees is mainly clouds. Its hazy appearance is caused by the appreciable atmosphere above the clouds. The highest deck of clouds is made of crystals of frozen ammonia. Farther down there are thought to be clouds made of frozen crystals of ammonium hydrosulfide and, at deeper levels, clouds of water ice crystals and ammonia droplets. All these chemicals are colorless when pure. However, the planet's clouds usually appear golden yellow-brown, perhaps because they also contain phosphorous compounds or some other chemical impurity.

In images captured by the Cassini spacecraft in the early 2000s, the atmosphere appeared blue in the northern hemisphere

and yellow-brown in the south. The blue region seemed to be relatively free of the yellow-brown clouds at the highest levels. The cloudless parts of Saturn's sky were likely blue for the same reason that Earth's sky is blue—molecules of gases in the atmosphere scattering sunlight in a way favoring shorter, bluer wavelengths. Scientists are not certain why the higher clouds appeared so much thinner in the north, but it may have been a seasonal effect. Later in the Cassini mission, as spring approached in the northern hemisphere in 2008, the atmosphere there began to turn less blue and more golden colored.

Like Jupiter, Saturn has alternating brighter and darker bands of clouds being pushed by east-west winds. Both planets also have swirling storm systems that appear as red, white, and brown ovals. The bands and ovals are less distinctive on Saturn, however, with much subtler color differences. This is partly because of the thick, partially transparent atmosphere above these features. Saturn's atmosphere is also less turbulent than Jupiter's. Occasionally, a very large storm erupts. These large storms seem to occur at about 30-year intervals, or about once each orbit. This suggests that they may be seasonal features. In addition, there are two huge cyclones apparently fixed in place, one at the north pole and the other at the south pole. The one at the north pole is surrounded by an unusual hexagon-shaped feature.

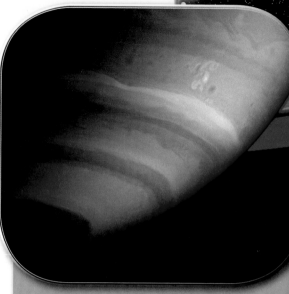

The bands of winds blowing eastward, in the direction of the planet's rotation, are vigorous. They alternate with bands of winds that are barely moving westward. Saturn's strongest winds blow eastward in a band over the equator from 20° N. to 20° S. Maximum wind speeds in this band reach nearly 1,100 miles (1,800 kilometers) per hour. Jupiter has a similar jet of winds near its equator, but Saturn's is twice as wide and its winds blow four times as fast. The fastest winds on Earth occur in tropical cyclones, or hurricanes, and are much slower. Only in extreme cases do they reach sustained speeds of more than 150 miles (240 kilometers) per hour.

Saturn is a stormy world. A giant thunderstorm called the Dragon Storm appears as a complex orange feature above and to the right of center in a false-color, near-infrared composite of images taken by the Cassini spacecraft. Scientists believe that it is a long-lived storm deep in the atmosphere that flares up from time to time. Lightning from the storm generates bursts of radio noise. **NASA/JPL/Space Science Institute**

Saturn's alternating bands of winds are remarkably symmetrical. Each band north of the equator usually has a counterpart south of the equator with about the same width and wind velocity. This suggests to scientists that the pairs of bands may be connected in some way deeper in the atmosphere.

The pressure increases with depth in Saturn's atmosphere. At the lower levels, where the pressure is extremely high, the hydrogen is probably crushed into a liquid. The temperature in the atmosphere also varies. At its coldest, it is about -312 °F (-191 °C). As on Earth, the temperature gets colder with altitude in the lowest level of the atmosphere but hotter with altitude in a middle level. In the highest level, the temperature is fairly constant.

INTERIOR

The temperatures and pressures in Saturn's interior are very high, and they increase with depth. As in Jupiter, the interior consists largely of hydrogen, which the immense pressure squeezes into a liquid. About halfway down between Saturn's cloud tops and center, the temperature is probably about 10,300 °F (5,730 °C). The pressure is thought to be some 2 million times greater than at sea level on

Earth. Under those conditions, the hydrogen is probably compressed into a liquid metallic state. In this state, the electrons are stripped away from the atomic nuclei, so the hydrogen would conduct electricity like a metal.

Saturn's central, liquid metallic region is denser than Jupiter's. Scientists have determined this by analyzing Saturn's gravity field. The planet's gravity is stronger at the poles than at the equator. The distortions in its gravity field are directly related to the relative amount of mass concentrated in its interior rather than in its atmosphere. This analysis suggests that Saturn's central regions are about half hydrogen by mass and half denser materials. Jupiter's central regions are thought to contain about two-thirds hydrogen and only one-third denser matter. Some of the denser material must be helium, which may be more concentrated in Saturn's interior than Jupiter's. Saturn's dense core is likely a mixture of rock and ice with about 10 to 20 times the mass of Earth.

Like Jupiter, Saturn radiates nearly twice as much energy as it receives from the Sun, mostly as heat. This means that the planet must generate some of its own heat. Much of this energy is probably left over from when the planet formed some 4.6 billion years ago.

Since then, the planet has slowly cooled down, gradually emitting heat. Scientists believe that some of the heat that Saturn produces probably comes from helium settling into its interior. It is thought that the helium separates out of the hydrogen and forms droplets, which sink toward the center. The friction of the droplets pushing against the other matter would create heat. This process is also thought to occur in Jupiter, but to a much lesser degree.

MAGNETIC FIELD AND MAGNETOSPHERE

Saturn's magnetic field is much stronger than Earth's but much weaker than Jupiter's. It has two poles, north and south, like a giant bar magnet. As on Jupiter, the orientation of the poles is opposite of that currently found on Earth. This means that a compass on Saturn or Jupiter would point south.

The planet's magnetic field dominates a large region of space called its magnetosphere. This region is shaped like a teardrop. The rounded part extends about 750,000 miles (1,200,000 kilometers) from the planet on the side facing the Sun. There, the magnetosphere holds off the solar wind, a flow of electrically charged particles from the Sun. On the side opposite the Sun, the solar wind pulls the magnetosphere out into an extremely long tail.

SPACECRAFT EXPLORATION

The first spacecraft to encounter Saturn was Pioneer 11. It was launched by NASA in April

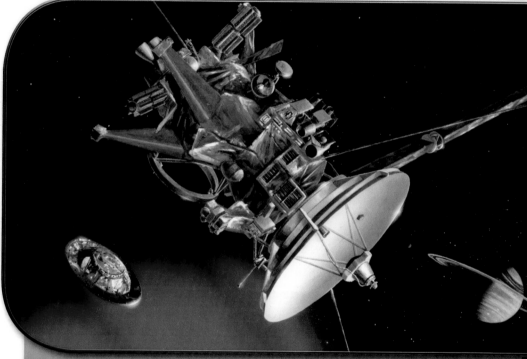

Artwork depicting the Cassini orbiter, center, after having released the Huygens probe, left, toward Saturn's moon Titan. The planet itself appears at back. The Huygens probe landed on Titan on Jan. 14, 2005, becoming the first craft to land on a solid body in the outer solar system. The Cassini craft began orbiting Saturn on June 30, 2004, returning a wealth of data and images about the planet, its rings, and its moons during a multiyear study. **NASA/JPL**

THE AURORAS OF SATURN

The inner part of Saturn's magnetosphere traps clouds of highly energetic protons and other electrically charged particles. The clouds travel around the planet in large regions called belts. These belts are similar to the radiation belts of Earth (called the Van Allen belts) and Jupiter. When charged particles collide with the hydrogen in the atmosphere above Saturn's poles, it causes glowing auroras, like Earth's northern and southern lights. Earth's auroras typically last only minutes. Saturn's, however, can last for days.

1973. After completing its original mission at Jupiter, the craft was reprogrammed and sent to Saturn. Pioneer flew within about 13,000 miles (21,000 kilometers) of Saturn's cloud tops in September 1979. It transmitted data and close-up photographs that enabled scientists to identify previously unknown moons, the F ring, and radiation belts within its magnetosphere.

NASA's Voyager 1 and 2 spacecraft, launched in 1977, were outfitted with more sophisticated equipment. After surveying Jupiter, the two spacecraft reached Saturn in November 1980 and August 1981, respectively. The Voyagers returned tens of thousands of images. The structure of Saturn's rings was found to be far more complex than could be seen in the lower-resolution Pioneer images or with the best telescopes on Earth. The craft also photographed previously unknown shepherd moons among the rings.

The Cassini-Huygens mission was launched in October 1997 as a joint venture between NASA, the European Space Agency (ESA), and the Italian Space Agency. The Cassini spacecraft began orbiting Saturn in June 2004 in order to study the planet, its moons, and its rings for several years. The orbiter carried on board the ESA-built Huygens probe, which it released toward Titan. The probe parachuted through Titan's atmosphere and landed on its surface in January 2005, providing the first look at the surface of the haze-shrouded moon. It transmitted data and photographs for about three hours during the descent and on the surface. It was the first craft to land on a moon other than Earth's. Among the discoveries of the Cassini-Huygens mission were a new radiation belt, a slightly longer rotation period for Saturn than previously measured, new moons, complex interactions between moons and rings, ice geysers on Enceladus, and methane rain on Titan.

CHARACTERISTICS OF URANUS

The seventh planet from the Sun is Uranus. It is one of the giant outer planets with no solid surfaces. Although Uranus is not as big as Jupiter or Saturn, more than 60 Earths would fit inside it. The planet is most similar in size and composition to Neptune, its outer neighbor. Like Neptune, Uranus is blue-green because of the

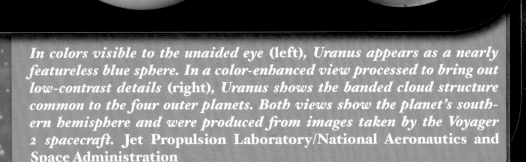

In colors visible to the unaided eye (left), Uranus appears as a nearly featureless blue sphere. In a color-enhanced view processed to bring out low-contrast details (right), Uranus shows the banded cloud structure common to the four outer planets. Both views show the planet's southern hemisphere and were produced from images taken by the Voyager 2 spacecraft. **Jet Propulsion Laboratory/National Aeronautics and Space Administration**

small amount of methane in its atmosphere, or surrounding layer of gases. Uranus orbits the Sun between the orbits of Saturn and Neptune. Like the other outer planets, Uranus has a system of rings and many moons.

Uranus was unknown to ancient astronomers. At its brightest, the planet is just barely visible to the unaided eye. It was seen in early telescopes several times but was thought to be just another star. In 1781, as part of a telescopic survey of the stars, English astronomer William Herschel discovered "a curious either nebulous star or perhaps a comet." This unusual object soon proved to be a planet, the first to be identified in modern times. It was later named

A montage of Voyager 2 photographs and artwork simulates a view of Uranus and its rings as if seen over the horizon of Miranda, one of the planet's major moons. Courtesy of the Jet Propulsion Laboratory/ National Aeronautics and Space Administration

Uranus, the personification of the heavens in ancient Greek mythology. Even with the more powerful telescopes available in the 21st century, the distant planet is difficult to observe in great detail.

WILLIAM HERSCHEL

The founder of modern stellar astronomy was a German-born organist, William Herschel. His discovery of Uranus in 1781 was the first identification of a planet since ancient times. Herschel developed theories of the structure of nebulas and the evolution of stars, cataloged many binary stars, and made significant modifications in the reflecting telescope. He also proved that the solar system moves through space and discovered infrared radiation.

Friedrich Wilhelm Herschel was born in Hannover, Germany, on Nov. 15, 1738. When he was 21 years old he moved to England to work as a musician and later taught music, wrote symphonies, and conducted. Herschel made observations of the sun at an early age but was 43 before he became a professional astronomer.

He discovered Uranus with the first reflecting telescope that he built. The discovery brought him an appointment as astronomer for George III, and he was able to spend all his time studying the stars. He was knighted in 1816. Herschel's observations of binary stars demonstrated that gravity governed the stars as well as the solar system. Herschel died in Slough, England, on Aug. 25, 1822.

SIZE, MASS, AND DENSITY

Uranus is the third largest planet in the solar system, after Jupiter and Saturn. Uranus is about four times bigger than Earth. Its diameter at the equator is about 31,763 miles (51,118 kilometers), as measured at the level of the atmosphere where the pressure is the same as at sea level on Earth. The planet is slightly larger than Neptune, but Neptune is about 1.2 times more massive. Uranus's density is quite low—only about 1.3 times that of water, compared with 1.6 for Neptune and 5.5 for rocky Earth.

ORBIT AND SPIN

Like all the planets, Uranus orbits the Sun in a slightly elliptical, or oval-shaped, orbit. With an average distance from the Sun of about 1,783,950,000 miles (2,870,990,000 kilometers), Uranus is about 19 times farther from the Sun than Earth is. The closest the planet ever gets to Earth is some 1.7 billion miles (2.7 billion kilometers) away. It takes Uranus about 84 Earth years to complete just one trip around the Sun. This means that a year on Uranus is about 84 times as long as a year on Earth.

A day on Uranus, however, is shorter than one on Earth. Uranus completes one rotation on its axis in about 17 Earth hours, compared with about 24 hours for Earth. This rapid rotation causes its polar regions to flatten slightly and its equator to bulge. The diameter at its poles is about 2 percent smaller than that at its equator.

Technically, Uranus spins on its axis in retrograde motion, or the direction opposite that of most other planets. However, it is a bit misleading to describe its rotation that way, because Uranus lies nearly on its side. Unlike in any other planet, its rotational axis is tilted an unusually large 97.9 degrees relative to the plane in which it orbits. Scientists think that Uranus may have been knocked into this alignment early in its history by one or more violent collisions with other bodies.

Each season on Uranus lasts about 21 Earth years. Because the planet is nearly tipped on its side, as it orbits it points first one pole toward the Sun, then its equator, and then the other pole. As a result, summers and winters are extreme, with one hemisphere bathed in sunlight for many years during its summer, while the other hemisphere is plunged in constant darkness for its long winter. The sunshine is more evenly distributed during spring and fall, when the equator is pointed toward the Sun. However, heat seems to be fairly evenly distributed year-round. The two hemispheres are probably always about the same temperature, probably because the atmosphere transfers and stores heat well.

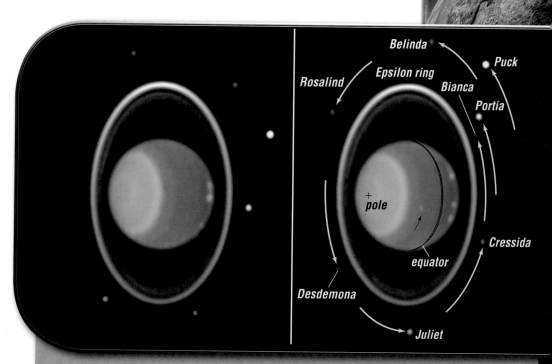

Uranus's southern hemisphere, ring system, and eight of its small inner moons appear in two false-color images made 90 minutes apart by the Hubble Space Telescope. Comparison of the images reveals the orbital motion of the moons along Uranus's equatorial plane and the counterclockwise rotation of clouds in the planet's atmosphere. **Erich Karkoschka, University of Arizona, Tuscon, and NASA**

RING SYSTEM

Uranus has a system of about a dozen narrow rings. Like Saturn's rings, they are made up of countless particles, each orbiting the planet like a small moon. The particles in Uranus's rings are much darker than those found in Saturn's bright, icy rings. Also, Saturn's rings have a much higher percentage of dust and tiny particles. Most of the objects forming Uranus's rings are larger than about 4.6 feet (1.4 meters) across. The small amount of dust in its rings seems to be constantly replenished. The dust may be knocked off small moons when objects hit their surfaces.

Two small moons, Cordelia and Ophelia, orbit on either side of one of the rings. The gravity of the two moons confines the ring particles into a narrow band, so they are called shepherd moons. Other small moons not yet discovered may also be shepherds for the other rings.

MOONS

Uranus has 27 known moons: five major moons and more than 20 smaller ones. The major moons, from nearest to farthest from Uranus, are Miranda, Ariel, Umbriel, Titania, and Oberon. Some of the small moons orbit near the rings, while others orbit beyond the major moons. The outer small moons are irregular, meaning that they have highly elongated or tilted orbits, or both. The inner small moons and the five major moons have nearly circular orbits that lie in about the same plane as Uranus's orbit.

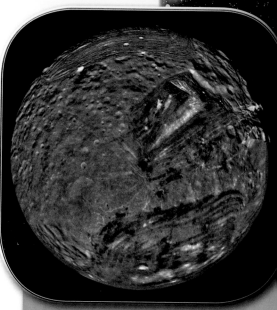

Miranda has the most diverse terrain of Uranus's moons. A mosaic of images taken by Voyager 2 shows the moon's south polar region, which has heavily cratered areas and large patches of lightly cratered regions marked with parallel bands and ridges. Such patches have not been found on any other body in the solar system. U.S. Geological Survey/NASA/JPL

The planet's five major moons range in size from Miranda, with a diameter of about 290 miles (470 kilometers), to Titania, with a diameter of some 981 miles (1,578 kilometers). The five moons are probably mostly water ice and rock. The four largest are thought to be about 60 percent ice and 40 percent rock. Miranda has a lower density, so it probably has a greater percentage of ice. The surfaces of all five major moons seem to contain dirty water ice. Umbriel and Oberon have many craters, large and small, like the highlands of Earth's

Moon. Like the Moon's, their large craters probably date back more than 4 billion years. Titania and Ariel have fewer large craters but about as many small craters. This suggests that Titania and Ariel have younger surfaces. Narrow canyons are found on all the major moons. They may have formed by the cracking of the crusts as the moons expanded.

Miranda has the largest canyons, with some being as much as 50 miles (80 kilometers) wide and 9 miles (15 kilometers) deep. Scientists think that all the water in its interior may once have been liquid. As the water froze, the moon would have expanded, causing the crust to fracture. Miranda has an odd jumble of different types of terrain. It mostly has heavily cratered, ancient surfaces. Other areas have fewer craters, sets of curving grooves, winding valleys, or steep cliffs. Miranda may have been broken apart by collisions with other objects and then reassembled to form the strange patchwork of terrains now observed. The different terrains may have formed instead by eruptions and other internal geologic activity.

PHYSICAL FEATURES AND EXPLORATION OF URANUS

L ike the other outer planets, Uranus has a massive atmosphere with a composition similar to that of the Sun and other stars. Much valuable information about the planet was gathered from close-up photographs and measurements taken in 1986 by Voyager 2, the only spacecraft to visit Uranus.

ATMOSPHERE

Scientists think that Uranus is roughly three-quarters hydrogen and one-quarter helium by mass, plus a small amount of methane and probably trace amounts of water, ammonia, and other substances. The highest clouds are quite bright and are formed of frozen methane. Farther down, there are perhaps clouds of frozen water and ammonium hydrosulfide. The lower parts of the atmosphere, in which clouds form, are quite cold, and the temperature there decreases with increased altitude. The coldest part of the atmosphere is about -366 °F (-221 °C). The temperature rises remarkably in the upper atmosphere, however, reaching 890 °F (480 °C).

very few features in
ASA/JPL

Unlike Jupiter and Saturn, Uranus appears nearly featureless in visible light. Faint bands of clouds are revealed in images taken at other wavelengths of light or processed to show extreme contrast. The bands of clouds are parallel to the equator. As on Earth and Neptune, winds travel west in a zone near the equator and east in zones at higher latitudes. The winds are several times stronger than Earth's but weaker than Neptune's. The atmosphere of Uranus seems to be calmer than those of the other outer planets. Spots observed on the planet are thought to be storms, but they are smaller and fewer than those seen on Jupiter, Saturn, and Neptune.

INTERIOR

Pressures and temperatures are extremely high inside the planet, so its interior must be liquid. Scientists think that Uranus is composed mainly of melted ices of water,

methane, and ammonia, with some molten silicate rock and metals, and a smaller amount of hydrogen and helium. At its center the planet might have a core of rock and metal. However, scientists think that the rock and metal are more likely to be spread throughout the fluid interior than in a separate layer.

The interior of Uranus is more like that of Neptune than like the interiors of Jupiter and Saturn, which are mostly hydrogen and helium. As in Neptune, melted ices, rock, and metal make up a much greater part of the mass. For some unknown reason, Uranus does not seem to generate as much internal heat as the three other outer planets. Those planets radiate almost twice as much heat as they receive from the Sun, but Uranus emits just a bit more heat than it receives.

Like most other planets in the solar system, Uranus produces its own magnetic field. It is similar to a bar magnet, with a north pole and a south pole. As on Earth, a compass would point north. However, Uranus's magnetic north pole is tilted an exceptionally great 58.6 degrees from its rotational north pole, compared with an 11.5-degree inclination for Earth. Only Neptune's magnetic field is similarly tilted.

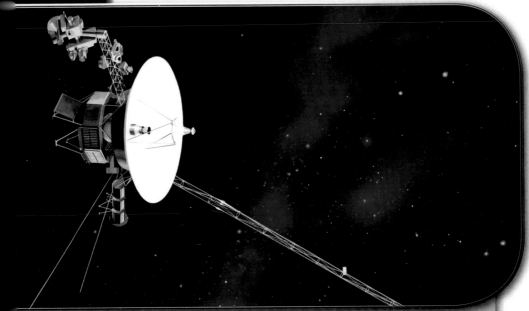

U.S. Voyager spacecraft, shown in an artist's depiction. The main body of the craft, located behind the large dish antenna used for communication with Earth, houses its navigation system, radio transmitters, and computers. Projecting above the antenna are cameras, spectrometers, and other instruments. The two thin rod antennas feed receivers that monitor planetary radio emissions and plasma-magnetosphere interactions. On the long boom (lower right) are magnetometers for measuring solar and planetary magnetic fields. The spacecraft's power source—three generators that convert the heat from radioactive isotope decay into electricity—occupy the canister between the rod antennas. **NASA/JPL/Caltech**

SPACECRAFT EXPLORATION

In August 1977 NASA launched the unmanned probe Voyager 2 on a mission to Jupiter and Saturn, with the hopes that it could later be sent to Uranus and Neptune.

The Voyager Probes

The mission of the interplanetary probes Voyager 1 and 2 was to observe and to transmit information to Earth about the giant planets of the outer solar system and the farthest reaches of the Sun's sphere of influence. Voyager 2 was launched first, on August 20, 1977; Voyager 1 followed some two weeks later, on September 5. The twin-spacecraft mission took advantage of a rare orbital positioning of Jupiter, Saturn, Uranus, and Neptune that permitted a multiplanet tour with relatively low fuel requirements and flight time. The alignment allowed each spacecraft, following a particular trajectory, to use its fall into a planet's gravitational field to increase its velocity and alter its direction enough to fling it to its next destination. Using this gravity-assist, or slingshot, technique, Voyager 1 swung by Jupiter on March 5, 1979, and then headed for Saturn, which it reached on November 12, 1980. It then adopted a trajectory to take it out of the solar system. Voyager 2 traveled more slowly and on a longer trajectory than its partner. It sped by Jupiter on July 9, 1979, and passed Saturn on August 25, 1981. It then flew past Uranus on January 24, 1986, and Neptune on August 25, 1989, before being hurled toward interstellar space.

On February 17, 1998, Voyager 1 overtook the space probe Pioneer 10 (launched 1972) to become the most distant human-made object in space. By 2004 both Voyagers were well beyond the orbit of Pluto. They were expected to remain operable through the first or second decade of the 21st century, periodically transmitting data on the heliopause, the outer limit of the Sun's magnetic field and solar wind.

After the spacecraft visited the two closer giant planets, its course was indeed changed to send it to the two outer giant planets. Voyager 2 became the first—and so far only—spacecraft to encounter Uranus, in January 1986, and Neptune, in August 1989.

After passing through Uranus's ring system, Voyager 2 flew to within about 66,500 miles (107,000 kilometers) of the planet's center. It measured the size and mass of Uranus and its major moons, detected and measured the magnetic field, and determined the rotation rate of the planet's interior. It took some 8,000 photographs at Uranus, including the first close-up images of the planet and its rings and moons. The images uncovered weather patterns in the atmosphere of Uranus and the surface conditions of the major moons; they also revealed for the first time many smaller moons.

CHARACTERISTICS OF NEPTUNE

The eighth and farthest planet from the Sun is Neptune. It is always more than 2.5 billion miles (4 billion kilometers) from Earth, making it too far to be seen with the unaided eye. It was the second planet, after Uranus, to be discovered through a telescope but the first planet to be found by people specifically searching for one. In the mid-1800s several astronomers began looking for a planet beyond Uranus, in part because Uranus did not move along its orbit exactly as expected. Scientists thought that these slight differences could be caused by the gravitational pull of another planet, and they were right. Several people can be credited with Neptune's discovery. John Couch Adams and Urbain-Jean-Joseph Le Verrier independently calculated the planet's probable location, while in 1846 Johann Gottfried Galle and his assistant Heinrich Louis

Clouds appear in Neptune's dynamic atmosphere in an image captured by Voyager 2 in 1989. At the center is the Great Dark Spot, a swirling storm system the size of Earth, and its associated methane-ice clouds. The giant storm system disappeared by 1991. **NASA/JPL**

d'Arrest were the first to identify it in the night sky. The new planet was named Neptune after the ancient Roman god of the sea.

Neptune's orbit lies beyond that of Uranus, the planet it most resembles in size and composition.

SIZE, MASS, AND DENSITY

Neptune is the smallest of the four giant outer planets. The diameter at its equator is about 30,775 miles (49,528 kilometers), as measured at a level of the atmosphere where the pressure is 1 bar (the pressure at sea level on Earth). This makes it slightly smaller than Uranus but nearly four times as big as Earth. Neptune's mass is about 1.2 times greater than Uranus's, however, and more than 17 times greater than Earth's. It is the third most massive planet in the solar system, after Jupiter and Saturn. Like the other outer planets, Neptune has a low density—only about 1.6 times the density of water. However, it is the densest of the four, being roughly 25 percent denser than Uranus.

ORBIT AND SPIN

Neptune revolves around the Sun in a nearly circular orbit at an average distance of about

2,795,083,000 miles (4,498,250,000 billion kilometers). On average, it is more than 30 times farther from the Sun than Earth is. Because of its great distance from the Sun, Neptune takes nearly 164 Earth years to complete one orbit. This means that one year on Neptune is 164 times as long as one on Earth.

The dwarf planet Pluto is usually farther from the Sun than Neptune is. About every 248 years, however, Pluto's highly eccentric (elongated) orbit brings it inside Neptune's orbit. Neptune is then farther from the Sun than Pluto is for a period of 20 years. It was last in this position in 1979–99. Pluto was classified as a planet from the time of its discovery in 1930 until 2006, when it was reclassified as a dwarf planet. So, for some 75 years, Neptune was considered the second farthest planet from the Sun.

Like the other gas giants, Neptune spins

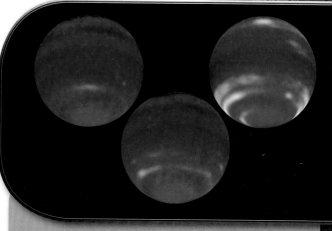

Seasonal changes in Neptune's atmosphere appear in images taken by the Hubble Space Telescope over six years during late spring in the southern hemisphere. The images were taken in visible and near-infrared light. They show bands of clouds in the south becoming wider and brighter as that part of the planet receives increasingly more sunlight. NASA, L. Stromovsky, and P. Fry (University of Wisconsin-Madison)

quickly, completing one rotation in about 16 hours. In other words, a day on Neptune lasts only 16 hours. The planet's rapid rotation slightly distorts its shape, making it bulge a bit at the equator and flatten a bit at the poles. Neptune's rotational axis is tilted about 29.6 degrees relative to the plane in which it orbits. As on Earth, the axial tilt gives it seasons. As the planet travels along its orbit, first one hemisphere, then the other is tipped closer to the Sun. Since Neptune's orbit is almost a perfect circle, its seasons are of even length, with each season lasting about 41 Earth years.

RING SYSTEM

A system of six narrow rings encircles Neptune. They are made mostly of dust-sized particles, all orbiting the planet. Arcs of brighter material punctuate part of the outermost and densest ring, called Adams. The rings are named after astronomers who discovered the planet and its important features. Inward from Adams, which lies some 39,000 miles (63,000 kilometers) from Neptune's center, are Galatea, Arago, Lassell, Le Verrier, and Galle, the innermost ring at about 26,000 miles (42,000 kilometers) from the planet's center. The four innermost moons of Neptune orbit within the ring system. At least some of them may be shepherd moons, whose gravity keeps the rings from spreading out.

MOONS

Neptune has 13 known moons. The largest, Triton, was discovered in 1846 by William Lassell only about a month after Neptune was discovered. With a diameter of 1,681 miles (2,706 kilometers), it is a bit smaller than Earth's Moon but a bit larger than Pluto. Triton is also similar to Pluto in density—both are about twice as dense as water—and surface composition. Frozen methane and nitrogen cover the moon's surface. At about -390 °F (-235 °C), it is one of the coldest known surfaces in the solar system. Triton's extremely tenuous atmosphere is composed mostly of nitrogen. Voyager 2 captured images of large, geyserlike plumes erupting. These active "ice volcanoes"

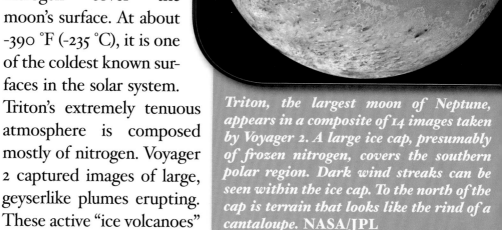

Triton, the largest moon of Neptune, appears in a composite of 14 images taken by Voyager 2. A large ice cap, presumably of frozen nitrogen, covers the southern polar region. Dark wind streaks can be seen within the ice cap. To the north of the cap is terrain that looks like the rind of a cantaloupe. **NASA/JPL**

THE UNUSUAL MOON TRITON

Unlike all the other large moons in the solar system, Triton revolves around Neptune in a direction opposite to the planet's rotation. Also, Triton's orbit is tilted more than 157 degrees relative to Neptune's equator, whereas most large moons are inclined less than about 5 degrees. These peculiarities suggest that Triton may have formed as an icy object elsewhere in the solar system and was later captured by Neptune's gravity. As its path was adjusted into a circular orbit, the pull of Neptune's gravity probably caused the moon's interior to melt and separate into layers. Triton later refroze.

likely spew nitrogen gas and large dust particles. Triton's average distance from Neptune's center is about 220,500 miles (354,800 kilometers). It completes one orbit around Neptune and one rotation on its axis in about 5.9 Earth days.

The distant moon Nereid was discovered in 1949, also by telescope. It has the most eccentric orbit of any known moon in the solar system. The moons Naiad, Thalassa, Despina, Galatea, Larissa, and Proteus were unknown until Voyager 2 visited the planet in 1989. They travel in nearly circular orbits that lie near the plane of Neptune's orbit. The other five moons were discovered by telescope in 2002–03. They are tiny outer moons with eccentric orbits that lie outside the plane of Neptune's orbit.

chapter 8

PHYSICAL FEATURES AND EXPLORATION OF NEPTUNE

The planet that Voyager 2 uncovered during its flyby of Neptune in 1989 is a stormy, windswept world with a vivid blue hue. Its highly active atmosphere is surprising, because it receives so little sunlight to power its weather systems.

ATMOSPHERE

Like the other outer planets, Neptune has a massive atmosphere, or surrounding layer of gases, composed mostly of hydrogen with some helium. Methane makes up most of the rest, accounting for about 2 percent of the molecules within the atmosphere. The methane gives Neptune its bluish color. Methane strongly absorbs red light, so the light reflected off the planet's clouds lacks red and appears blue. Uranus has a similar percentage of methane, but it appears blue-green. Some other substance that has not yet been identified must give Neptune its more vivid blue color.

Temperatures vary with altitude in Neptune's atmosphere. At a point where the pressure is 1 bar, the temperature is about

Neptune's clouds appear in thin bands, much like Earth's cirrus clouds. **NASA/Ames Research Center**

-326 °F (-199 °C). Above that point, it gets colder with altitude in a middle layer but warmer with altitude in a higher layer. The highest levels of Neptune's atmosphere are quite hot, with a constant temperature of some 890 °F (480 °C). Temperatures vary with altitude in Neptune's atmosphere. At a point where the pressure is 1 bar, the temperature is about -326 °F (-199 °C). Above that point, it gets colder with altitude in a middle layer but warmer with altitude in a higher layer. The highest levels of Neptune's atmosphere are quite hot, with a constant temperature of some 890 °F (480 °C).

Air currents in the atmosphere probably rise at middle latitudes and descend near the equator and poles. Near the cloud tops, the winds blow east-west in zones, as on Jupiter, Saturn, and Uranus. Near Neptune's equator, the winds whip westward at some 1,570 miles (2,520 kilometers) per hour, the fastest wind speed ever found in the solar system. At higher latitudes, the winds blow eastward at slower speeds.

The highest clouds in Neptune's atmosphere appear in delicate bands like Earth's

NEPTUNE'S GREAT DARK SPOT

Voyager 2 detected considerable atmospheric turbulence during its 1989 flyby. An enormous, whirling, Earth-sized storm system called the Great Dark Spot appeared as a dark oval in photographs of Neptune's southern hemisphere. A smaller dark spot and a bright, fast-moving cloud called Scooter also appeared. Unlike Jupiter's Great Red Spot, however, which is at least 300 years old, Neptune's large storm systems do not seem to be long lasting. The Great Dark Spot did not show up in images made with the Hubble Space Telescope just a couple of years after the Voyager flyby. Another dark spot appeared for a few years in the planet's northern hemisphere in Hubble images taken in the 1990s.

cirrus clouds. They are probably formed of crystals of frozen methane. These high, dispersed clouds cast shadows on the main cloud deck below, which may be formed of crystals of frozen ammonia or hydrogen sulfide. Cloud layers probably exist below the main deck, including some likely made of water ice.

INTERIOR

The pressures and temperatures inside Neptune are exceptionally high, so the interior is probably liquid. Scientists think it is

made mostly of melted ices of water, methane, and ammonia plus molten silicate rock and metal. It also contains a smaller percentage of hydrogen and helium. Neptune's composition is most similar to that of Uranus. Because Neptune is denser, it is thought to contain a greater percentage of the heavier substances — the molten rocky material and melted ices. Scientists doubt that Neptune has distinct layers like Jupiter and Saturn. Instead, the heavier substances are probably well mixed throughout the fluid interior, as in Uranus.

Like Jupiter and Saturn, Neptune radiates roughly twice as much energy as it gets from the Sun, for some unknown reason. It seems to have a strong internal heat source. The planet is more than a billion miles (1.6 billion kilometers) farther from the Sun than Uranus is, and it receives less than half the sunlight that Uranus does. Nevertheless, Neptune is slightly warmer than its inner neighbor.

Neptune produces its own magnetic field, which has a north pole and a south pole, like a bar magnet. However, the north magnetic pole and the north rotational pole are skewed. Neptune's magnetic field is tilted almost 47 degrees relative to its rotation axis. Only Uranus's magnetic field is tilted more. This configuration may indicate that processes in the upper layers of the interiors, and not the centers, generate the magnetic fields in both planets.

SPACECRAFT EXPLORATION

The unmanned NASA probe Voyager 2 is the only spacecraft to have visited far-off Neptune and its moons. In August 1989 the craft flew past Neptune, observing the planet and its moons for several months. Its closest approach took it only about 3,100 miles (5,000 kilometers) above the planet's north pole. The data and the some 10,000 photographs it obtained substantially increased knowledge about Neptune and Triton, confirmed that the planet has rings, and revealed for the first time six of its moons. The mission also detected the planet's magnetic field and surprisingly high-speed winds and active storms in the atmosphere. After the Neptune flyby, Voyager 2 was hurled toward interstellar space.

Neptune (far left) Uranus, Saturn, and Jupiter. NASA

CONCLUSION

Astronomers have been able to gather considerable data on the four giant outer planets thanks to recent improvements in Earth-based observational technology. However, the greatest advances in scientists' knowledge of these planets have come from deep-space probes. Much of our knowledge about Uranus and Neptune was learned in the 1980s from a single spacecraft's observations, Voyager 2, during its flyby of the two planets. Despite the huge achievements of exploratory missions, many questions remain unanswered. Only future space probes will be able to address them. The Galileo mission provided images and other data related to Jupiter's moon Europa suggesting the presence of a liquid water ocean beneath its icy crust. Future missions will seek to confirm the existence of this ocean and search for evidence of organic or biological processes in it. Astronomers also hope to more thoroughly investigate the extensive systems of moons and rings found on the outer planets. These systems may hold vital clues to the origins of the planets themselves—as well as to the origin and evolution of the whole solar system.

anticyclone A system of winds that rotates about a center of high atmospheric pressure clockwise in the northern hemisphere and counterclockwise in the southern hemisphere.

asteroid Any of the small rocky celestial bodies found especially between the orbits of Mars and Jupiter.

aurora Streamers or arches of light appearing in the upper atmosphere of a planet's magnetic polar regions caused by the emission of light from atoms excited by electrons accelerated along the planet's magnetic field lines.

flux tube A cylindrical region of space containing a magnetic field.

friction The force that resists relative motion between two bodies in contact.

gossamer rings Faint rings, such as the rings of Jupiter, composed of thinly distributed particles.

magnetic field The portion of space near a magnetic body in which the magnetic forces caused by the body or current can be detected.

magnetometer An instrument for measuring the strength and sometimes the direction of magnetic fields, including those on or near the Earth and in space.

magnetosphere A region of space surrounding a celestial object that is dominated by the object's magnetic field so that charged particles are trapped in it.

nebula Any of numerous clouds of gas or dust in interstellar space.

probe A device used to penetrate or send back information, especially from outer space or a celestial body.

radiation Energy radiated in the form of particles.

retrograde motion Having or being motion in a direction contrary to that of the general motion of similar bodies and especially east to west among the stars.

shepherd moons Moons that help produce rings around a planet by pushing particles together as they orbit.

spectrometer An instrument used for measuring wavelengths of light spectra.

trajectory The curve that a body (as a planet or comet in its orbit or a rocket) describes in space.

tributary A stream feeding a larger stream or a lake.

wavelength The distance in the line of advance of a wave from any one point to the next point of corresponding phase.

Amateur Astronomers Association of New York
P.O. Box 150253
Brooklyn, NY 11215
(212) 535-2922
Web site: http://www.aaa.org
An organization devoted to helping amateur
    astronomers keep up with the space
    program, learn what's happening at the
    frontiers of astronomical research, and
    appreciate the beauty of the night sky.

Griffith Observatory
2800 East Observatory Road
Los Angeles, CA 90027
(213) 473-0800
Web site: http://www.griffithobs.org
Griffith Observatory is a national leader in
    public astronomy. The observatory fea-
    tures the Samuel Oschin Planetarium,
    telescopes, and on-going exhibits in
    astronomy.

Hayden Planetarium
Central Park West at 79th Street
New York, NY 10024
(212) 769-5100
Web site: http://www.haydenplanetarium.org
The Hayden Planetarium operates out of
    the Department of Astrophysics at the

American Museum of Natural History. Its mission is to bring the frontier of space and astrophysics to the public via exhibits, books, public programs, and on-line resources.

H.R. MacMillan Space Centre
1100 Chestnut Street.
Vancouver, BC V6J 3J9
Canada
(604) 738-7827
E-mail: info@spacecentre.ca
The H.R. MacMillan Centre is a nonprofit community resource. The center inspires interest in the universe, Earth, and space exploration through innovative programming, exhibits, and activities.

National Aeronautics and Space Administration (NASA)
The Space Place
New Millennium Program Education and Public Outreach
Jet Propulsion Laboratory
Mail Stop 606-100
4800 Oak Grove Drive
Pasadena, CA 91109
Web site: http://spaceplace.jpl.nasa.gov/en/kids/index.shtml

NASA's Space Place is a joint effort by
the NASA Jet Propulsion Laboratory,
California Institute of Technology,
and International Technology and
Engineering Education Association. It
was launched in February 1998 as a learn-
ing and community outreach program.

Royal Astronomical Society of Canada
203 - 4920 Dundas Street W
Toronto, ON M9A 1B7
Canada
(888) 924-7272
Web site: http://www.rasc.ca/
The Royal Astronomical Society of Canada is
the country's foremost astronomy organization. It unites amateurs, educators, and
professionals and offers local programs
and services throughout Canada.

WEB SITES

Due to the changing nature of Internet links,
Rosen Educational Services has developed an
online list of Web sites related to the subject
of this book. This site is updated regularly.
Please use this link to access the list:

http://www.rosenlinks.com/tss/oute

Benton, Julius. *Saturn and How to Observe It* (Springer, 2006).

Fischer, Daniel. *Mission Jupiter: The Spectacular Journey of the Galileo Spacecraft* (Copernicus, 2001).

Irwin, P.G.J. *Giant Planets of Our Solar System: Atmospheres, Composition, and Structure,* 2nd ed. (Springer, 2009).

Leutwyler, Kristin. *The Moons of Jupiter* (Norton, 2003).

Lorenz, Ralph, and Mitton, Jacqueline. *Lifting Titan's Veil: Exploring the Giant Moon of Saturn* (Cambridge Univ. Press, 2002).

Lovett, Laura, and others. *Saturn: A New View* (Abrams, 2006).

Miller, Ron. *Uranus and Neptune* (Twenty-First Century Books, 2003).

Rothery, D.A. *Satellites of the Outer Planets: Worlds in Their Own Right,* 2nd ed. (Oxford Univ. Press, 1999).

Spangenburg, Ray, and Moser, Kit. *A Look at Jupiter* (Watts, 2001).

Standage, Tom. *The Neptune File: A Story of Astronomical Rivalry and the Pioneers of Planet Hunting* (Walker, 2000).

Tocci, Salvatore. *A Look at Uranus* (Watts, 2003).